The Road Warrior
A Sales Manual

Mike Swedenberg

Author of The Sales Rep Survival Guide

ISBN-13: 978-1511466691

ISBN-10:1511466693

DEDICATION

Boopa, thank you for the love and support.

Harley, Hudson and Quinlan, never ever give up, no matter what!

.

CONTENTS

"Don't just sit there, go out and sell something."

- From the Greatest Quotes of Mike Swedenberg

ACKNOWLEDGMENTS

To all of my good managers who taught me the right way and the bad

managers who made me appreciate the good ones even more.

.

Forward

The problem with most how to sales books is that they spew theory and impressive words and expect you to bask in all their wisdom. It makes sense to them because they have done it for years. However, for the average person who has to make a living selling goods and services without the help of a full time sales manager, it's impossible.

I have worked for Fortune Fifty companies including Procter & Gamble, Johnson & Johnson and global publishers that have on-going sales training. I have also worked for Mom & Pop outfits that can barely understand what it is they do themselves much less ever explain it to a new sales person. They offer a choice of three training programs:

LOYO: Learn On Your Own

YOYO: You're own Your Own

And the ever popular FIOFY: Figure It Out for Yourself because if the owner tries and teach you, then you will realize exactly how little he knows about what he sells.

I was once selling for a small company and asked the sales manager a question about our product. He was the owner's son who graduated from a two-year community college with a degree in communications. He looked at me with annoyance and said, "It ain't rocket science." That's when I knew I was on my own.

This book covers the basics in simple language. No frills no fluff, but it's up to you to read, absorb and make it work. You may email me at Michael.swedenberg@gmail.com with any questions.

My experiences include selling directly to professionals, consumers, to retail stores and wholesale. Here is a list of products and services I've sold.

Advertising print, displays and signs

Law books

Health and Beauty Aids

Pharmaceuticals (The legal kind)

Food

Water filtration

Copiers, Faxes and cell phones

CHAPTER 1

Plan Your Work and Work Your Plan

Cold Call vs. Sales Call

I have been in jobs that use the term sales call or cold call to mean different things. To some, a sales call is when you pick up the phone, call prospects and try to sell them a product or get an appointment to come by and sell them in person.

In my world, cold calling is going out in the field and knocking on doors looking for new business. A sales call is visiting a current customer to write new business or for customer service. When I sold books to lawyers, the reps were not allowed to sit in the office to make cold or telemarketing calls. That was "Dialing for Dollars." We had to be in the field 100 percent of the time and if we needed to phone a client, we did it from the field from a pay phone or cell.

In another job the reps were not allowed to set foot outside the office unless we had a confirmed appointment using the Outlook calendar and copying our boss.

Either way, you need to be prepared to make the call and have a set action plan. This way you don't get side tracked or forget to do stuff that will cost you a sale.

Tip: Customers hate being called customers. Call them clients and treat them like one.

CHAPTER 2

SEVEN STEPS OF THE CALL FOR RETAIL SALES

You need to decide what steps you take when you make a sales call and do them until you know them by heart. Skipping steps will cost you sales. These are the steps I used when I sold to grocery and drug stores. They apply to almost any situation.

Step 1. PLAN YOUR CALL. Know who you will see, how you will get there and what you will sell them. Have a suggested order in case you meet the buyer walking out as you walk in. You can hand him or her a suggested order that you prepared ahead of time and ask if you can stop in later. Have a brochure with your card and details of the product or service in your hand. Spending twenty minutes a day writing up suggested orders for each of your planned calls isn't really a hard thing to do. If it gets you just one extra order a week, what would that do to your income?

If you meet the client in a hallway, parking lot or standing next to the receptionist, you can sell them if you are prepared. I've written many orders on the spot. Always acknowledge the client's valuable time. Walk with him or her down the hall and say, "Hi Ms. Jones. I'm (your name). I can see you're in a hurry. May I leave you this brochure? I believe it will help you in your business. I will get back to you at two o'clock to follow up." Don't ask if you may see the client at two o'clock, say you will be back.

Think positive as though the client is interested. Don't give them the chance to say "No." Once they say "No," selling them is harder and in a hallway presentation, there is no time to overcome objections. Instead, focus on what time you will come back, not if they want the product. The client may say "No" again. Assume that they disapprove of the time, not the product. Then ask, "Would three o'clock be better?"` A Hallway Presentation is used to sell an appointment. Then you come back and sell your widget.

Step 2. Say Hello. At some point of the sales call, you must introduce yourself to the client. In many industries, there are things to do before you make a presentation, like taking inventory. Before you do that, take a moment to say hello to the buyer and let him or her know you're there. They will expect you when you come back for a presentation.

Years ago, when I was a front end pharmacy manager, I had a route salesman walk up to me and hand me a bill for an order he had just written. He had been in the store for twenty minutes taking inventory and building a display. I had been pre-occupied with something else and didn't know he was in the store. He was angry when I told him to tear down the display because we had postponed the promotion for a month. If he had found me first and said hello, I could have saved him a lot of wasted time and bad feelings. Perhaps he thought this was a good way to sell or perhaps he didn't think at all.

Simply put; let the buyer know you're in the store or office before you proceed with the call. If the store manager says he doesn't have time to see you, ask if it's alright to check the shelves and inventory and that you will come back later. Leave a suggested order when you leave. That way, most of your work will be done when you return.

Tip: Always ask permission before you do anything in a store or client's office.

Step 3. CHECK INVENTORY. Nothing is more embarrassing than to give a retail store buyer a presentation and suggested order, only to have them say that there are thirty cases of your product in the back room. You would have seen it if you had bothered to look. You may think that they don't have any inventory, but they may have bought your merchandise from a wholesaler since your last visit. Taking inventory also allows you to look for "out of stock" situations, competitive activity and empty areas for displays.

In cases where you sell office equipment, instead of taking inventory, you do an on site inspection. You take the time to look at traffic flow, volume needs and special requirements. When you make your presentation, you have a greater understanding of the buyer's needs and can recommend the proper stuff.

Whatever the type of selling you do, taking inventory or stock of the situation makes you look like you know what you're doing. You aren't just there to sell something; be a consultant to help resolve problems. Treat your buyers like clients rather than customers.

You can get great information by checking their web site. Folks love to boast about all the things they do and have on their website because it boosts their ego and it's free. It's not like they have to pay for fancy brochures every year. If you were a buyer what would you rather hear from a sales rep?

1. Do you need a box of widgets?

2. I looked at your website and see you sell widgets. We offer a premium widget at a great price. May I show you?

Step 4. PRESENTATION. Refer to the next section for the five steps of the presentation.

Step 5. MERCHANDISING. Whether you write an order or not, you may have an opportunity to merchandise the product you already have in the store or office. This could entail building displays, point of purchase merchandising, cleaning an existing piece of equipment, or talking with the accountant to rectify a past due invoice. Do this after the order is written. The buyer may leave or no longer have time to see you if you delay the presentation.

Step 6. PAPERWORK. Do your paperwork, while the information is fresh in your mind. This includes call reports, changes of phone numbers or personnel changes. You will forget important details if you wait until the end of the week. The file you're creating will be totally useless. Do your paperwork after each call and your paperwork will be done by the end of the day. When I sold law books, I'd ask the lawyer if I could use his fax machine to fax in the order; they always said yes. It was a toll free number back when you paid for long distance calls. It cost them nothing.

Technology changes at a rapid pace and you may be able to use a scanner, iPad or similar device to transmit orders. Keep in mind that my sales career began in 1980 when orders were snail mailed to order processing. By 1986, the pharmaceutical company I worked for gave us laptop computers to manage our territory and transmit orders. In 1992, I worked in legal publishing that still used hand written account cards and we faxed our sales orders to the office. In 2000, another publisher only accepted orders that were phoned in. Regardless of the tools available, at the end of the day, my paperwork is done. Your situation may be different. You may use a computer, scanner or smart phone to place your orders. Doesn't matter, do it right away and get it done.

Step 7. THINK ABOUT THE CALL. This is an important mental step. As you drive or walk to your next call, reflect on the success or failure of the last call. Think about each step of the call. What did you do that was right or wrong? Were there things that the buyer said that you didn't act on? When you find something new and useful, try to repeat it on the next call.

GIVING A BASIC PRESENTATION

OPENING STATEMENT

The purpose of an opening is to start a conversation. When cold call canvassing, you need to introduce yourself, your company and the purpose of your call.

An example would be:

"Hello. My name is_____ and I'm with _____, the number one manufacture of_____ in the United States."

Our product can reduce your costs due to a 6 percent reduction in electric power needs and increase your production with a 15 percent increase in productivity. I need only four minutes to explain the system in general terms. At that point, you can determine a need for further discussion. "May we talk now?"

Let us examine each section of the opening:

"Hello. My name is_____ and I'm with _____. We are the number one manufacture of_____ in the U.S."

This tells the client who you are, what company you work for and the success your product has achieved. I never mention my title sales rep or account manager or any of the other titles companies use. That sends a red flag up in the client's mind. Instead of thinking about what you're saying, they are wondering what you're trying to sell them and how they can get rid of you. This isn't a presentation. The purpose is to open lines of communication.

"Our product can reduce your costs and increase your production due to a 6 percent reduction in electric power needs and a 15 percent increase in productivity."

Your product delivers this benefit to the client. This is relevant if the client has older, less efficient equipment and that saving money and increasing productivity is a goal of his. To determine what things to say about your product or service in an opening, see the following section on "Features and Benefits."

"I need only four minutes to explain the system in general terms. At that point, you can determine the need for further discussion."

You aren't there to waste their time and the decision to continue discussion is entirely theirs. I use an odd time like four minutes because everyone says, "I only need five minutes." I once had a prospect take his desk clock and turn it around so we could both see it. He said, "OK, you now have three minutes and fifty-three seconds." I was able to finish in time.

Practice your short hallway presentation, time yourself and use that time frame. Stick to your word! Don't ramble and don't try to get into a full presentation until part four of the opening and the buyer says, "This would be a good time, right now."

"May we talk now?"

Ask if you may begin the first part of the sales call known as probing. You don't ask if they want to buy the product. You ask if you can take time now to begin discussion of the product. This assumes that they are interested and are deciding if now is a good time. As an alternative, use the "Strategy of Choice."

If the buyer seems busy, then offer a choice of time: "Would now be a good time? How about two o'clock?" They then decide WHEN, not IF they want to see you. Use the "Strategy of Choice" throughout the sales process. A cold call becomes a set appointment. You have a reason to return and the buyer is expecting you.

PROBING

Probes are questions you ask the client about their needs and objectives BEFORE you begin a presentation.

I received a phone call at home from a woman who launched into a prepared script about the oil heat company she represented. She spoke quickly and was obviously reading. She talked about the low cost, free service contract and free burglar alarm given to each new customer. The spiel went on for about a minute and concluded by asking if a sales representative, who just happened to be in the neighborhood, could stop by. I believe she delivered the entire presentation without once taking a breath. I politely declined.

"And why not?" She asked.

"I have gas heat," I replied.

"Oh. Thanks for your time sir."

Tip: DON'T ASSUME; ASK! Because when you ASS/U/ME, you make an ASS out of U and ME.

Never ASSUME that everyone is looking for the lowest priced item. They're not. Do you look for the cheapest pair of shoes or those that fit, look and wear well? I had a client insist he only buys the cheapest products he can find and we were too expensive for him even though he admitted he need it. He was wearing a diamond encrusted Rolex as he spoke. I asked if price was a concern, why he didn't buy a $30 Timex instead. They both do the same thing; tell you the time of day. His office was filled with expensive furniture and equipment and that told me price wasn't his only concern. He eventually bought from me but it was a tough sale and I had to justify our costs.

Never ASSUME that everyone is unhappy with his or her present service and are holding their breath for you to show up. Some people have dealt with the same supplier for years and have had many reps try to switch them. Others simply hate change. It's too much bother, even if it means a few extra dollars in savings.

Never ASSUME that everyone is willing to drop what they are doing and make a snap decision because you walked in the door just so you can make your sales quota.

Depending on your product and service, you may approach probing in different ways. You must find out what the clients' needs and goals are. They may not know that they have needs. It's your job to uncover them and then provide a product or service to resolve those needs.

When I sold health and beauty aids to grocers and drug stores, I generally had to ask only one probing question before I gave my presentation. "If I could show you how to increase your volume and profit, would you be interested?" Volume and profit are two goals I knew from experience that my clients wanted to achieve. Depending on the marketplace, they may wish to achieve higher volume at the expense of profit or vice versa; however, most would like to achieve both simultaneously.

If I sold synthetic motor oil, I could ask a car owner, "Would you be interested in increasing your miles per gallon and your horsepower without spending extra money?" To say no would make the owner look stupid.

Two important guidelines when probing:

1. Know the answer before you ask the question. If I'm selling an attorney a set of books for an area of law he normally doesn't practice, I may ask: "Counselor, are you tired of sending clients to your competition?"

2. Deliver on your promises: "We have a great set of law books on New York State Wills that take you through the process step by step. This will enable you to retain new clients who may bring you more important work in the future. Besides, if you keep sending your client to another attorney, next time they have a problem, who are they going to call, you or the last attorney who helped them?"

Tip: Don't ASSUME professionals are the best business people. They may be a great lawyer, pharmacist or doctor but have trouble running a Kool-Aid stand without adult supervision.

When detailing pharmaceuticals, you ask the physician a series of probing questions. When I sold an antifungal cream, to dermatologists, (skin doctors) I had a prepared list of thirty probes. I asked five or six from the list below, before I began my presentation.

I could tailor the presentation to the doctor's specific needs and expectations.

Here are some of those probes I used:

"What type of fungal infections do you see?"

"How do you like to treat them?"

"Are you always pleased with the results?"

"Is cost ever a factor?"

"How many cases keep coming back?"

"What do you do then?"

"What product have you been using?"

"Does it always work to your expectations?"

"Tell me what the ideal antifungal would be like."

Even if you don't know anything about drugs, you should get the drift of my questioning. Each question sets the stage for my presentation. I developed my probes based on my product's features and benefits. My product had distinct advantages over the competition and before I begin my presentation, I have the doctor's attention focused on these key areas.

Reps who sell photocopiers would ask questions about the client's copier needs. They ask about traffic flow, number of employees and so forth. Once they gather the information, the reps can tailor their presentation to the specific needs of the client. They would emphasize the relevant features and discount the irrelevant ones. If the client indicated that the bulk of the copies made are single sheets, there would be little use in presenting the built in stapler. On the other hand if the client needs six page reports, the stapling feature becomes an important selling point. Why present a feature the client can't use?

A rack jobber selling snacks may ask the store manager about traffic flow or clientele. "Is there a busy office or a high school nearby?" That would help the buyer decide how to position the display and what snacks to stock. If the store sells a lot of cold soft drinks, the jobber would want to place the rack near the soda machine for strong tie-in sales. It drives me nuts when I walk into a convenience store to buy a soft drink and then have to walk around looking for the pretzels. I feel like screaming at the owner: "Put a stupid display of snacks by the soda, for crying out loud." I understand that retailers spread thing around the store to encourage you to shop around. This drives impulse sales, but it still drives me nuts.

For other types of products and services, look at the features and benefits and use them to help build a list of probing questions. As you gain experience, you will add new ones and discard others.

Tip: Never be afraid to ask clients about specific problems of their business. It shows your desire to learn about their needs and goals

There is a difference between asking a prospect about his specific needs and asking the buyer for the Acme Refrigerator Door Magnet Company, what kind of products they make. One makes you look like a pro, the other makes you look lazy and stupid. Can you decide which is which?

Use the Internet to learn about your prospects. Go to their web page and look under the About Us and the Our Services tabs. Publicly held companies issue annual reports that detail their products and services. Sometimes, there are catalogues available in the waiting room. The more you know before you walk in the buyer's office, the better your chances of selling stuff.

I read a survey few years ago that said the biggest beef buyers had were with reps that start out, "Can you tell me about your business?"

Tip: Never ask clients general questions about their business unless you are unable to find it. Do your homework.

During probing, you will run across prospects that are loyal to your competition. Focus on your major advantage, for instance, price. The competition and you both have a good product but yours is 20 percent less expensive. The magic bullet to use is: "If you could change one thing about the product you're now using, what would it be?"

You know the answer is cost, but you have brought it up in such a fashion that it is the client, who exposes the competitor's major weakness, not you. For you to say, "The competition charges too much," you invite the client to defend his purchasing decision. He or she might say, "They are a few dollars more, but I get great service." By asking an open-ended question, you allow the client to verbalize the objection to the competition.

Tip: Never criticize your competition. It's unprofessional and the prospect may come to their defense.

A potential client, one I had been unsuccessful in meeting, called to set an appointment. He told me my competition had been in and spent fifteen minutes bashing my product and service. The client was so curious, that he had to see for himself how bad we were. He discovered that our product was indeed better. He didn't like dealing with an jerk and thought that we must be doing something right to make our competitor nervous. I want to thank the rep for the order I got that day.

Sometimes reps are tempted to criticize their competitors. Consider this actual conversation between a buyer and a sales rep that I overheard.

As the rep walked through the factory floor, he stopped a worker and pointed to his competitor's equipment.

"Well, who's the idiot who bought the Acme Roto machine?"

"Me! I'm the idiot." The worker said.

"Didn't you realize that our Mr. Roto machine cost less and is faster?"

"I had other considerations."

"Boy that was a big mistake. I bet you regret it now."

"See the #!@&##@ door?"

"Yes."

"Leave!"

This isn't an exaggeration. I've heard otherwise good reps openly criticize a buying decision without realizing they were talking to the decision-maker.

Imagine if you drove in to a car dealership and wanted to trade your pride and joy in for a new car. How would you feel if the salesman asked: "I can't believe you bought a Dorkmobile. Let me show you our new Coolride." Would that put you on the defensive? Would you be open to deal with that salesman?

This is pride of ownership. I've never sold anything that I didn't have confidence in. I understand my competition and know the distinct advantages of my product over theirs. The greatest danger of bashing the competition, especially if the client is presently using it, is that you're indirectly telling the client that they made a mistake. The buyer will defend his or her decision making process. It's bad form to point out someone else mistake, especially when you're trying to sell them something.

At one publishing company, my advantage over my competitor was in price and format. We approached a legal issue differently. My job was to get attorneys to cancel their subscription to other publishers and to subscribe to mine.

When I presented books to an attorney who had the competing set, I said: "The set you own is a great publication. I've taken time to review it, and I can see its many advantages." I've reinforced the attorney's buying decision. By complimenting my competitor, I take the high road.

I then say, "We have taken a good idea one step better," or my magic bullet, "If you could change one thing about the set you now subscribe to, what would it be?"

The door is open if client mentions cost. If the client doesn't raise the cost issue, it's O.K. to bring it in the back door as a benefit during your presentation: "Counselor, The benefits to our publication are one, two, and three. In addition our set is inexpensive to maintain. What are you presently paying?" (I already know the answer.)

Tip: Never ask a question about cost unless you already know the answer.

CLOSED END QUESTIONS

These are probing questions used to get either a yes or no answer. Avoid closed ended questions when you're probing to discover of a client's business or buying habits. They should ONLY be used in the close.

Examples are:

Are you prepared to make a decision today?

Are you interested in our service?

Do you prefer to pay cash or credit?

When you ask a closed end question, you may get an answer you aren't looking for, such as:

"Are you happy with your current supplier?"

"Yes I am."

Even if the client isn't happy with his current supplier, he may be reluctant to admit it, because you are a "pesky salesman" and will try to sell him something. It's easier to say "No!"

OPEN ENDED QUESTIONS

These are probing questions that request more than a yes or no answer. Use them DURING the presentation. They can generate a wealth of information.

Examples are:

Can you tell me about your business cycle?

What type of customers do you see most often?

What type of problems have you experienced in the past?

Keep your open-ended question to two or three; don't give your client the third degree. If your open-ended question generates interesting information, but not enough for your presentation, you may ask: "Can you tell me more about that?"

FEATURE VS BENEFIT

One of my managers, John, had a great way to explain the difference between a feature and a benefit.

"If you say something about your product and the buyer asks, 'SO WHAT?' it's a feature. If he says, 'WOW!' It's a benefit."

A feature is an aspect of your product or service. An example is that you sell an on-line investment software program that allows you to buy and sell stocks. One of the many features is a "Customized Daily News Update." (SO WHAT?) The benefit is what that feature will do for your client. The Daily News Update sends you an e-mail on any stock splits, earnings reports and mergers. You can customize it for any stock, mutual fund and news item you prefer. This gives you valuable information that occurred overnight that would affect your investment before the market opens. (WOW!)

Bill is a sales representative trying to sell a shop supervisor one case of disposable ballpoint pens for use in the warehouse. Bill is talking about features; however, the shop supervisor is listening for benefits. See if you can tell when the sales rep stops talking "SO WHAT" and starts talking "WOW."

"Mr. Stevens, unlike any other disposable pen, our ball point pen has a pressurized ink cartridge."

"So what?"

"The ink is kept under constant pressure." Bill replies.

"So what?" Stevens asks again.

"The ink flows at a constant rate."

"So what?"

Bill wondered why the supervisor didn't get it. After all, he has given this presentation a hundred times; the benefit is perfectly clear. The rep tried to make it simpler.

"The air pressure in the cartridge forces the ink toward the ball point at all times."

"So what?"

Bill thought to himself, this guy is thick as a brick; any idiot can see the benefit. I better spell it out for him. Bill continues, "The benefit is that the pen will write at any angle, even upside down. So when you're making notes on a clipboard hanging on the wall, or lying on your back while entering an inspection number to the bottom of a machine, the pen will always write. You don't have to stop every few seconds and shake the pen to make it work."

"Wow! Why didn't you say so before?"

"I thought I did." Bill quips.

"Send me five cases at once,"

Tip: Just because the benefit is obvious to you, it's not always obvious to your client.

When self-winding watches debuted about sixty years ago, the benefit was self evident to anyone who wore a watch. As long as you wore it, the movement of your arm kept the watch wound. Perhaps the mechanics weren't widely understood but you knew you no longer had to wind the watch every day to keep it running.

In the 1970's when the first quartz appeared, the benefit of a battery-operated watch wasn't obvious. People believed it to be a variation of a successful product that was more accurate since that was the way the company advertised it.

The benefit was that the watch would continue to run even if you took it off and left it on the dresser for a year. That was something a self-winding watch couldn't do. The advertising only stressed the accuracy. The benefit wasn't self evident to the public.

In the late 1980's, long after the quartz watch was introduced, I met a rep at a training class who wound his quartz watch every morning before class.

"Why are you winding a battery operated watch?" I asked.

"I didn't know it had a battery. Aren't you supposed to wind it everyday?"

"Nope. It's like an electric clock."

"I've wound it every day for the last year and it works fine," he said defensively.

"All you're doing is spinning a watch stem that isn't attached to anything except the gears that adjust the hands. It has no mainspring. There is nothing to wind," I said.

It wasn't until I removed the battery and his watch stopped that he understood the benefit of a quartz watch.

He wasn't the only one who didn't see the obvious. I used a word processor for six months before I discovered what "Spell

Check" was. I would type a letter, and then review it with a dictionary to check my spelling.

CHAPTER 3

THE 5 STEPS OF THE PRESENTATION

The presentation is a sales tool that allows for a two-way conversation between a seller and a buyer. It isn't a one-way conversation where the seller talks and the buyer just listens. Think of a presentation as a radio transmission. A one-way conversation is when you listen to a radio broadcast in your home. It's not interactive. They talk and you listen.

A two-way conversation is like a conference call. Both you and the person on the other end talk to each other. It's interactive.

Tip: All presentations should be a two-way conversation.

ASERT and The Five Steps of a Presentation

ASERT is an acronym:

Get the buyers' Attention.

Say what you want.

Explain it.

Review the benefits.

Trial close.

As with many aspects of successful selling, there are steps involved in the presentation. You should progress through the steps in order. Memorize them and they will become part of your thought pattern. You can then expand the system of ASERT to every aspect of sales and negotiations including direct mail advertising.

ATTENTION

First, get the buyers' attention. Say something to peak their interest enough to make them stop what they are doing and devote a few minutes to what you have to say.

I've written an example of each step of the presentation for someone selling a floor standing display of candy to a retail store. You will see cardboard floor displays in a pharmacy or supermarket standing in the aisle filled with merchandise like snacks, candy and shampoo.

For this example, you should know that dead space is any area of the selling floor that isn't producing income for the store. If a store has five-hundred square feet of floor space and they are paying $2,000 per month in rent, each square foot is costing them $4 per month. If the owner puts a candy display on the floor, it will generate income and the space it occupies will be "live." That is why manufacturers design their retail floor displays to fit into one square foot. (Also known as the footprint.)

ATTENTION: "I can convert one square foot of dead space in your store to $50 worth of profit a month."

SAY WHAT YOU WANT

It's important to tell the buyer up front exactly what you want to do. Instead of paying attention to what you're saying, the buyer will be trying to figure out what you're selling and how to get rid of you.

Say what you want: "My idea is for you to put this display of candy in your store."

EXPLAIN IT

Explain exactly how the program works. With experience, you will learn to anticipate objections. Address as many of them as possible in this step.

Explain it: "Here is how it works. My candy is a proven winner. We have more than seventy-five displays in this county alone. At full markup, and a volume of only one-hundred pieces a month, which is the average, you will generate $50 a month in profit. The attractive display takes up one square foot of space and holds six cases of assorted candy. The candy is rotated on a monthly basis and is a guaranteed sale." (A guaranteed sale means the store gets full credit for any unsold inventory.)

"I will build the display, clean and refill it each month. There is no obligation or contract to sign; if you ever decide you want it out, just call and I will pick it up."

Never say your product is cheap. Say it's less expensive. Cheap can mean crappy quality in your clients mind.

REVIEW BENEFITS

Emphasize what is in it for the store. Emphasize the benefits not features. The benefits to you are:

"You will turn one square foot of wasted space in to a profit center. You will generate $50 in profit per month. The attractive display will encourage impulse sales and put more dollars in your register. It's a guaranteed sale and I will maintain and clean it as well."

TRIAL CLOSE

A close is when you ask for the business. This is a trial close because you haven't finished with the presentation. In most cases, you will have to overcome objections before the buyer makes a decision; however, a trial close will indicate the interest level and may result in an early sale.

Trial close: "Ms. Jones, I have a display rack in my car and can have it set up in fifteen minutes. How about that dead space by the second cash register?" (Don't ask IF she wants the rack; ask WHERE she wants the rack.)

Another trial close is giving the buyer a choice in quantity, "How about two racks instead of one? We can put one in the candy aisle and the other by the register."

Hint: You know there is a space for the display near register number- two because you followed step three of the sales call and found a space before you made your presentation.

Following are other examples of ASERT:

Example 2

ATTENTION: "I can increase your volume and profit without you spending any money."

SAY WHAT YOU WANT: "My idea is for you to move our product off the bottom shelf and place it at eye level."

EXPLAIN IT: "Here is how it works: Any product sells faster at eye level. Since we have a higher volume (or profit) than our competitor, you will benefit by placing us at eye level.

REVIEW THE BENEFITS: "The benefit to you is an increase in volume and profit."

TRIAL CLOSE: "Is now a good time?" If the buyer says no, then ask, "How about first thing tomorrow?"

Example 3

ATTENTION: "We can increase your productivity and still show a 6 percent savings in overhead."

SAY WHAT YOU WANT: "My idea is for you to purchase our high speed photocopier."

EXPLAIN IT: "Here is how it works: Our copier is faster than any other on the market. This results in less time your staff has to wait in line to make copies. Our superior quality results in lower down time and that's how you achieve an increase in productivity. You achieve a savings in overhead because our machine requires 6 percent less energy to run."

REVIEW THE BENEFITS: "The benefit to you is higher productivity and lower overhead."

TRIAL CLOSE: "We can have the machine delivered and running by Friday. Is that soon enough?"

Example 4

ATTENTION: "Doctor, would you be interested in an effective drug that can be used once a day versus the twice a day one you're now prescribing?"

SAY WHAT YOU WANT: "My idea is for you to prescribe my new drug on your next ten patients. This way you can see for yourself how good it is."

EXPLAIN IT: "Here is how it works: Our drug isn't absorbed through the skin, therefore only has to be applied once a day vs. twice a day as in the drug you're now prescribing. You can help your patients save money by prescribing a smaller size tube."

REVIEW THE BENEFITS: "The benefit to you is that you give your patients a good drug that's easier to use and saves them money."

TRIAL CLOSE: "Will you prescribe our drug for the next ten patients who need it?"

Example 5

<u>ATTENTION</u>: "How would you like to stop sending your clients to your competition?"

<u>SAY</u> WHAT YOU WANT: "Counselor, my idea is for you to expand your legal practice into a new area."

<u>EXPLAIN</u> IT: "Here is how it works: Stop sending people who ask you to prepare wills or trusts to other attorneys. Our treatise takes you through each step of preparing simple wills and trusts. We also include the forms on computer disk. You simply pull the will up on your screen and fill in the blanks. This set will pay for itself the first time you use it, the rest is increased profit and these new clients may ask you to represent them in other areas as well."

<u>REVIEW</u> THE BENEFITS: "The benefit to you is you increase your revenues and future potential."

<u>TRIAL</u> CLOSE: "Would you like me to send the books third class mail? What if I send them express mail at my expense?"

Example 6

<u>ATTENTION</u>: "I can reduce your inventory levels without costing you any money."

SAY WHAT YOU WANT: "My idea is for you to build a display of your back room inventory in a high traffic area."

EXPLAIN IT: "Here is how it works: Displays, set up in high traffic areas of your store, increase the number of sales of that item by 250 percent. By taking the merchandise out of the back room and placing it on display, you will lower your inventory and increase your sales. You won't have to spend any money on labor since I will do the work for you."

REVIEW THE BENEFITS: "The benefit to you is you lower your back room inventory and put the cash in your register faster."

TRIAL CLOSE: "I have the time to build the display now. Is that O.K., or do you prefer this afternoon?"

Fact: No sales rep ever died from asking for the business

There are sales reps that think it is undignified to ask someone to buy something from them. Reps should find their own comfort level in sales; but I think you're just plain nuts if you don't ask for the business.

These reps think they have done their job by getting into the buyer, uncovering needs and making a good presentation. Then it is up to the client to express an interest in making a purchase.

When I was in my early twenties, I worked part time during the holiday rush at Macys in Roosevelt Field, on Long Island. I worked in the men's department with a woman who was assistant manager. When a customer expressed interest in a sweater, I didn't ask if she wanted to buy it, I asked, "Would that be cash or credit?" More often than not, I made a sale. As we walked to the register, I would stop at the shirt rack and say, "Hey, this shirt would go nicely with this sweater, would you like that too?" Many times I made a multiple sale.

The assistant manager, Ms. Thumble, pulled me aside and said, "That is the wrong thing to do. You are a clerk, not some kind of fancy salesman. Don't be pushy."

"I just make suggestions. I don't twist anyone's arm. I ask the customer once, if they say no, I just drop it." She was adamant and finally, one night, I said, "Ms Thumble, look at the register at the end of day. You always have about $600 in receipts and I have more than $1,500. Isn't that the purpose of being in business?"

That was my last week at the department store. The manager said Ms. Thumble found me difficult to work with and too pushy.

I heard a great story on sales from one of my managers. Frank was an insurance agent and he spoke of a yearlong relationship with a potential client, named Tom. They met often for golf and had a great personal relationship. Frank waited patiently for Tom to ask him to sell him life insurance. Frank recounted how devastated he was when Tom bought policies for his employees from another agent.

"Tom, after all of this time we have known each other, why did you buy insurance from a stranger?"

Tom seemed surprised at the question and replied, "Well Frank, you never asked me. The other agent showed up one day, made a presentation and asked me to buy the policies. I needed a new agent because I was unhappy with my old one, so I said yes."

"Tom, this won't affect our friendship; but, you knew I was in the insurance business."

Tom shrugged and said, "Of course, but all we ever talked about was family and golf, you never once mentioned insurance. I ASSUMED you didn't think your policies were right for me and that is why you never asked."

Remember: If you don't ask, you don't get.

CHECKING

Checking simply means that you ask for input from the buyer during the presentation. This keeps the buyer's attention focused on what you're saying. After mentioning a feature / benefit, you ask, "How does that sound?" Wait for a response, either a yes or a nod.

Other checks include:

1. "Does that sound helpful to you?"

2. "Would that be beneficial?"

3. "Does that sound fair?"

Checking also opens the door for trial closes. If the response is, "Yes, that's exactly what I need!" then skip the rest of the presentation and go directly to a close. "Great! I can have it shipped in this Friday. Is that soon enough?"

A TIME TO SHUT UP

When you finish your presentation, ask for the business and then SHUT UP. The rule is: The first person, who talks, loses.

This is a game of nerves. You have asked Mr. Smith to purchase ten cases of your product. You sit eyeball to eyeball. He waits a few minutes, while he thinks over his decision. DON'T SAY A WORD! I don't care how thick the tension is or how great the temptation. DON'T SAY A WORD! The buyer has won if you do. DON'T START REPEATING YOURSELF. It's a sign of insecurity. If the buyer talks first, the business is yours. The only questions remaining are how much and how soon.

Zeke, my manager from Hell, never grasped this concept. When we worked together, I would ask the buyer for the business and then shut up. Zeke was unable to stay quiet for more than five seconds. He would start the presentation all over again. We rarely wrote any business when we worked together.

I tried to tell Zeke what I was doing, but he wouldn't listen, nor would he do what I asked. After all he was a "sales manager" and to him reps were just "scum of the earth."

Once, he interrupted my silent treatment and blew a major presentation. Afterwards, I politely said, "Zeke, I'm the sales rep. This is my territory, and I'm ultimately responsible for the success or failure of it. Please don't interrupt during a presentation. When I ask for the business and then shut up, I'm using a strategy that has worked very well for me in the past."

Zeke replied, "You are bordering on insubordination. I'm the manager and I will do as I please."

I never took Zeke to an important client again.

I've seen reps talk themselves into a sale and promptly talk themselves out of one, simply because they wouldn't shut up.

I was watching a sales rep present a promotion to a store manager that involved one-hundred cases of shampoo for a large end cap display. He gave a competent presentation, overcame several objections, found a great spot for the display and asked for the business. The buyer was running in circles trying to unload a truck and said, "OK, send it in."

Instead of shutting up and writing the order, the rep kept selling. He brought up new topics about the promotion he hadn't mentioned before. This generated more questions from the buyer. The rep tried to answer them but succeeded only in placing a seed of doubt in the buyers mind. In a matter of moments, the buyer changed his mind. "Ya know what? Let me think about it. Call me on Friday and I will let you know what I will do."

I never saw the display in that store.

TIP: When the client says yes, SHUT UP and write the order, You won.

LISTENING

One of the most difficult things I had to learn as a sales rep was to listen to the client. One training class I went to was a great exercise for developing this important skill. We each choose a partner, sat face to face and told each other our life story in about one-hundred words or so. We had to rely on our memory and couldn't take notes. We then had to stand in front of the class and describe the other person's life. Our partners could correct us if we made a mistake.

We continued this around the room until we had met with everyone. That day, during role-play, we gave presentations to each other in front of the class and had to throw in the personal information we had learned. This forced us to concentrate on what the other person was saying.

When our manager worked in the field with us, we would pause after each call, and repeat everything that had happened during the call. This is part seven of the Seven Steps of the Call, Analyzing the Call. This included whom we met, their names, their positions, any small talk, the presentation, the buyer's reactions and any questions asked.

In the beginning, it was difficult and frustrating. However, as I gained experience, I learned to recount the entire sales call in total.

My boss would say, "Mike, during the presentation you mentioned the special sale and the buyer said last time he sold out early. You went ahead and suggested the same quantity as before. You know you should have increased your suggested order. Did you not hear him or was this some sort of secret strategy?"

The fact was I heard him say that and recalled it clearly, once my manager mentioned it. I focused so much on delivering my presentation that I didn't pay attention to what the buyer was saying.

If you work for yourself and have only me as a trainer, I suggest you sit in front of the TV and listen to the evening news. At the end of the broadcast, recount how many details you can recall. Either tape the show and replay it or have someone take notes and ask you questions.

STRIKE WHILE THE IRON IS HOT

Many times a client will give you a buying signal that indicates he's sold. You must listen carefully and be prepared to act quickly to take advantage before he changes his mind.

When I was a pharmacy manager, a sales rep called on me and launched into a product presentation. Although he did no probing and apparently spent no time looking the store over, I wanted to place an order.

It was for merchandise that I'd been trying to locate. Several times during the presentation, I gave a buying signal.

"OK, that sounds good, when can we get it?"

"In about three days," he answered, then continued with his presentation

Again, I gave him a buying signal: "That would be great. I've been looking for those. What is the minimum order?"

"No minimum, whatever you need is fine." He continued with his presentation.

I interrupted with another buying signal; "Can I get a display rack? I would like to put it in our window for a sale."

He nodded, "Yeah sure, whatever you want." He finished his presentation, handed me his card and said, "Well, maybe next time," then promptly left the store.

I followed him outside to stop him. "What's the problem? Aren't you going to write an order?"

He looked at me and said, "You didn't say you wanted the stuff."

"Yes I did, three times?"

He came back in, somewhat puzzled and wrote the order.

He was transmitting his message on a one-way radio. He couldn't pick up my buying signals and if it wasn't for me chasing him down the street he would have lost an order. I wasn't playing head games with him. I was a busy manager carrying on a normal conversation. Since I didn't grab him by the collar and shake him, he thought I wasn't interested. Don't make your clients smack you in the head with a 2x4 so they can buy something.

Tip: If you're halfway through a presentation and the client gives you a buying signal, use a trial close. If the client says yes, shut up and write the business.

In the case where you have misunderstood his signal, the buyer will let you know: "Not so fast, I need more information," or something to that effect.

Examples of buying signals include:

"That will be fine."
"Sounds good to me."
"When can I get it?"
Specific questions about quantity, delivery, prices or promotional support are all buying signals.

CHAPTER 4

OVERCOMING OBJECTIONS

The fun begins when the buyer says, "NO."

Well not really, but one of my sales trainers told me that back in the day and it stuck in my head. It's no fun at all when a buyer says no. It means no commission for me and I can't reclaim the time I spent making the sales call. However, not all is lost. There are ways to save a percentage of these lost sales.

When a buyer says "No." you have the opportunity to distinguish yourself from most sales reps in the industry.

Believe me when I tell you, based on my thirty-five years in sales, there are precious few who know how to overcome objections. Most just argue with the client, or worse, pack up and walk out of the door.

Of all the aspects of this book, this chapter is the most important and this section is the most critical.

A buyer says "No" because he or she has a reason not to buy from you. It's your job to uncover that reason and overcome it.

The thirty-three reasons buyers say "No."

1. No room.

2. Wrong product or service.

3. Wrong clientele.

4. The buyer is satisfied with his present supplier.

5. The buyer doesn't see the need.

6. The buyer is lazy either intellectually or physically – maybe both.

7. The buyer thinks it is too big for their needs.

8. The buyer is in a hurry to go home.

9. The buyer had a fight with the spouse that morning.

10. The person you think is the buyer has no authority to place an order.

11. His boss told him not to place any orders.

12. Your competitor is the buyer's brother-in-law.

13. You have bad breath.

14. The buyer doesn't like your tie.

15. You rub the buyer the wrong way.

16. The buyer thinks he can negotiate a better deal.

17. The buyer never says yes on the first try.

18. The buyer doesn't understand you.

19. The buyer is in a bad mood.

20. You messed up the last order.

21. The buyer thinks you're arrogant. (Some confuse confidence with arrogance.)

22. The buyer isn't convinced you understand his needs.

23. The buyer thinks you're a crook.

24. You are a crook, and the buyer knows it.

25. The buyer thinks you want to sell something they don't need or want.

26. The buyer hates all sales reps.

27. The buyer is stupid.

28. The buyer is smart, but thinks you're stupid.

29. It's the wrong day of the week.

30. He or she has no reason; but, simply loves to give "pesky salesmen" a hard time.

31. You remind the buyer of another rep he or she hates.

32. The buyer is mad at your company.

33. The buyer is jealous. He/she believes all sales reps are under worked and over paid.

Now, look at that list of objections. Do you think you have the time or patience to go over each one of them to determine which objection he or she has and then overcome it? You would be lucky to make two calls a day.

I dramatically increased my success level by asking the buyer, "What is the main reason you won't buy this product?" I will describe this multi-step process in detail.

FALSE OBJECTIONS

You have given your presentation to a store manager for a display of cologne. You asked for the business, shut your mouth and waited.

The buyer scratches his head and says, "No!"

"May I ask why not?" you ask politely.

Tip: The first objection out of the buyer's mouth is probably a false objection.

We hear and give false objections during the course of the day. Someone asks you a favor and you think of an excuse to say, "No." You don't want to hurt their feelings by telling them the true reason, so you offer a plausible excuse.

A clerk in a store flags you down in the aisle to show you a new line of sweaters. You smile and politely refuse, "Sorry, not today. I'm in a hurry." The truth is you have plenty of time; you just think the sweaters are hideous. You know if you stop and look you will feel guilty if you don't buy one. You are a nice person and you don't want to hurt the clerk's feelings. A false objection avoids confrontation.

After presenting a display to a store manager, he says, "No."

"May I ask why not?" (Do so politely don't sound confrontational or sarcastic.)

"I don't have any room in my store for your display."

The truth is he has plenty of room. If you offered him a display filled with $10,000 worth of merchandise absolutely free, he would manage to find room for it. However, you can't challenge him by saying, "Oh yes you do, right over there. What's the real reason you won't buy from me?"

WARNING: Never challenge a buyer. You must be diplomatic at all times.

NEVER IGNORE AN OBJECTION

When a buyer says, "We have no room," acknowledge the objection. Never challenge it or dismiss it. Doing so won't remove the objection; it will only drive it underground. It's better to acknowledge the objection by saying, "I understand. Space is a problem in your store."

FOLLOW UP

Ask the buyer: "Is there any other reason you can't buy the display?"

He may answer: "Well I think it has too much merchandise in it for my volume store."

Acknowledge: "I understand your concern with overstock." (Don't try to overcome the objection yet.)

Follow up again: "Is there any other reason?"

He may say: "Yes, it is too much work to build the display once it comes in."

You acknowledge again: "I see, well is there any other reason?" (Don't try to overcome the objection yet.)

I hope at this point, he will say: "No, that's about it."

NOW DISCOVER THE TRUE OBJECTION

Instead of trying to answer each objection, simply ask which of the three objections is his real concern. "Well, let's see, you're concerned with space, the amount of inventory and building the display. Of those three things, what is your biggest concern?"

Such a question not only acknowledges the buyer's objections but also illuminates the real concern. The buyer may say, "Well I'm worried that the display has too much inventory and it will take to long to sell through."

CONFIRM THE TRUE OBJECTION. DON'T RESPOND YET!

You can determine if that's the true objection by asking, "Well if I resolve that problem, will you reconsider and take the display?" You have challenged the buyer, but not in a threatening manner. When the buyer says, "Yes," then you know that's his real objection. You don't have to address the other two reasons.

If the buyer says, "No, even if you resolve that problem, I still won't buy the display." You haven't uncovered the true objection.

Tip: Don't waste time answering false objections.

OFFER A RESOLUTION.

The true reason was the amount of inventory.

You respond, "We have a smaller display with half as much inventory. Why don't we bring that one in instead?"

Now that you have offered a resolution to the concern, the buyer says, "OK, send it in."

IF THE BUYER STILL SAYS NO

You asked the right question, "If I resolve that problem, will you reconsider?" If the buyer says, "No!'" there maybe more than one objection. Start the process over.

"What else is on your mind?"

The buyer may say: "I don't have space, even with a smaller display."

You confirm again, "I understand. If I can find room for a smaller display, would you take it?" The buyer may say yes if those are the two real objections. Again, it is important to have followed the seven steps of the call. You already have scoped out the store and have found several good spots for the display. "There is a great spot in aisle four by the shaving cream. It would fit nicely there and be a great tie-in profit maker." You have succeeded. The buyer says, "Send it in."

This works because you took time to uncover the buyers concerns and needs. You weren't there to just sell him stuff and run out the door. And believe me, that is exactly what many sales people do.

At Procter & Gamble, I covered Manhattan. It was a walking territory since I could not park on many of the city streets. The Health & Beauty Aid stores, pharmacies and grocers I sold to numbered in the hundreds all jammed into an island three miles wide and nine miles long. My accounts were located close to each other and we reps tripped over each other during the course of the day. Once a rep with a competing company introduced himself to the buyers with the same line, "I'm in a sales contest and I only need one more display to win a trip to Florida." He said that at every store we called on that day. The message he transmitted was clear. He was there not to help the store make money, but to win a contest for himself. Once, I could believe, but he said it at several accounts. It was obvious he was lying. At some point that approach is no longer effective. In my career, I overheard others use the same opening statement. Put yourself in your accounts position. You see twenty-five sales reps a week and three guys are always trying to win a sales contest. What would you think? Who would you put your trust in?

Tip: Be a consultant instead of an insincere fly-by-night hustler. . Help your clients solve problems, grow their business and make money. It never gets old.

CHAPTER 5

IT'S SIMPLE

You can often close a borderline buyer with simple communication skills. You will succeed where others fail because they gave up too easily or got caught up trying to answer each objection as fast as the buyer threw them out. As you gain experience, you may even increase your success rate.

If you have followed these steps, overcome the objections and the buyer still says no, don't get frustrated. You haven't done a bad job. Sometimes objections can't be overcome. It's time to move on. Sell it to his competition across the street.

Once when I was in legal publishing, I tried everything I could to sell a nationally acknowledged set of law books to an attorney. I demonstrated that our set was recognized by the court and was more up-to-date than the competition. All the attorney could focus on was the price. We were several thousand dollars more than the competition. I could not overcome this objection. I packed up my sales bag and moved on. Several months later, the lawyer called our customer service department and placed an order for that set of books. He made it clear that he did not want to speak to me directly. I learned of this when I got credit for the sale on my next commission report. Later, I got a call from another attorney who thanked me for selling him the same set of books. He was in court against the first attorney. The opposing counsel has cited my competitor's set. The second attorney objected, citing that my set noted the case in question had been recently overturned and therefore was bad law. The other attorney lost the case causing him embarrassment and his client a large sum of money.

PRODUCT KNOWLEDGE

I never appreciated the importance of product knowledge until I was in pharmaceuticals. I had to study my products thoroughly and have a basic understanding of human anatomy. It didn't stop there. I had to know the competitors' products to the point that I could sell them. This included their chemical compounds, how the drug affected the human body and how it treated the disease.

Professionals, like doctors, lawyers and accountants are detailed oriented. Before you can modify their habits, you must demonstrate your knowledge and expertise in that area. This is more than memorizing a few features, benefits and advertising slogans. It involved constant reading of trade journals, discussions with product managers and conversations with the clients.

You may sell a product that doesn't lend itself to extensive product knowledge. When your client isn't the end user, he doesn't care which product is best, only if he can resell it to someone else. As an example, a drug store buyer won't care how your therapeutic hand lotion works, only how much it costs and how fast it sells. A dermatologist, on the other hand, is very concerned with the product's efficacy and details of its contents. He won't care about the profit margin or sales volume.

You may substitute industry knowledge and marketing knowledge for product knowledge if you're in that situation. Read trade journals, clip out articles you find relating to your product and use them during your presentation.

Your drug store buyer may not care how your product works and won't be motivated to buy it based on its therapeutic value. However, show him an article from a trade journal that shows the growth of the product's marketplace and your brand's market share and you will demonstrate your knowledge and expertise. This works whether you are selling expensive merchandise or bags of candy. As an example, your product has a 20 percent market share and the store you are calling on does not stock your brand. You demonstrate how much business they are loosing to loyal clients who want your product. If the store says they don't have room on the shelf, you use the market share numbers to show that they are giving 15 percent of the shelf space to a competitor who only has a 5 percent market share. You suggest that they cut down on the number of facings (number of rows) that product has. Use that freed shelf space and inventory dollars to stock your brand. That way, the store can grow their volume and profit without spending more money. That is what a consultant does. A "pesky salesman" will try to force the product on the store without justification.

If you don't have access to this marketing data, find a large store or national chain and see how they merchandise the products. They do have access to marketing data and rest assured that if a product has 15% of the shelf space in that section, it's because they've earned it. There are always exceptions to the rules. You may have an ethnic or regional product that has unique market share. Your company may have specific information you can use instead.

EPILOGUE

I've tried to open a new door of opportunity for you. It's now up to you to walk through. Sales is an easy way to make a good living and affords job security found in only a few professions.

I could lose everything today, my home, my savings and all of my possessions. Move me across the country to where I had no friends or business contacts and in sixty days I would receive my first commission check. Within six months, I would be back on my feet and within a few years I would be back to my former level, if not greater.

You may be a better sales representative than me. You may be smarter, better educated, more experienced and have a better personality; but, I will earn as much - if not more because I will work longer and harder than you.

Let's say you can document that you're twice as good a sales representative as I am. You need to work only forty hours a week to earn

$100,000 a year. In the same job, I will earn $150,000 per year because I'm willing to put in sixty hours a week.

God made each of us different - but He gave us time as the great equalizer. Put in the time and you will surpass everyone else on the playing field. Put in the time and you will succeed.

THE 46 COMMANDMENTS OF SALES REVISED

1. Watch out for number one. You are number one and no one else will care for, or attend to your success more than you.

2. Always cover your ass. Document everything in writing.

3. Work harder and smarter. The days of simply working smarter, not harder are gone forever.

4. Don't get mad or even. Life is too short to waste on anger and revenge. Learn from the transgressions of others and go on with your life.

5. Kill 'em with kindness. Overcompensate for your mistakes and they will be quick to forgive and forget.

6. Keep 'em talking to discover the truth. A liar can't keep track of his deceptions for long.

7. Give it to 'em straight. The truth is always easier to remember.

8. Ask for the business and then shut up. There is a time to talk and a time to be quiet. Put the burden on their shoulders.

9. Never criticize the competition. Take the high road and acknowledge their success. You may work for them one day.

10. Beware of New Manager Syndrome.

11. It's not what you have; it's what people think you have. Right or wrong, people still judge others by the cover of their book.

12. Address a problem when it happens. When ignored, it will fester and grow in proportion.

13. Never argue with a client. You will win the battle and lose the sale.

14. Never drink on the job.

15. Beware of the gossip. When he talks about others behind their back, he's talking about you behind yours.

16. Charm will carry you for about fifteen minutes, after that, you better know your stuff.

17. There is no excuse for bad manners.

18. Never discuss religion, politics or sex with a colleague or buyer. You will inevitable step on someone's toes.

19. Believe in the 60/40 rule. In most situations, 60 percent of the people will go one way and 40 percent will go their other way.

20. Believe in the 25 percent rule. 25 percent of the people you meet won't like you for any number of reasons.

21. Believe in the 100 percent rule. Those with money, prefer 100 percent natural products.

22. Don't assume-ask. When you ass/u/me, you make an ass out of u and me.

23. Make fun of yourself not others. No one will ever argue with you if you point out your obvious shortcomings, but they will come to the defense of others.

24. Follow the style not the trend. The style is dependable; the trend fades by evening.

25. Never burn your bridges. You never know when your old contacts will crop up next.

26. Never condemn others in public. To do so will make you look bad and will illicit sympathy for your opponent.

27. Never be afraid to ask questions. It shows your concern for others.

28. Always try to resolve problems yourself. When your boss has to do your job, he doesn't need you.

29. Admit your mistakes. Never defend the indefensible.

30. Speak positively of your employer.

31. Always have fun. Don't take life too seriously. Enjoy the fruits of your labor.

32. Put yourself in your client's shoes. Practice total empathy. Would you buy something from you?

33. Don't get distracted from your goals. Treat each hurdle and roadblock as another step to your goal that you didn't anticipate.

34. Always take a vacation. No one can be on stage all of the time.

35. Understand the rules. You will be a mile ahead of the competition.

36. Quality doesn't guarantee success. Your product may be the best, but that doesn't mean it will be number one.

37. Nothing sells itself. Companies need salespeople to take their message to the customers.

38. Always bird dog. Pay others to open doors for you.

39. When it works, keep doing it. Nothing beats a system that brings results.

40. Remember, if sales were easy, they wouldn't need you.

41. Do someone a favor long enough and they will come to expect it.

42. You can't make money sitting in a coffee shop. Get in front of your client.

43. It's not how much you make. It's how fast you make it.

44. Never dwell on your failures; look forward to your next success.

45. Get up one more time than you fall down.

46. Time is not money. Time is time and money is money.

Good luck and great selling.

Mike Swedenberg

Glossary

ASSORTED DISPLAY: A dump bin or display table in which an assortment of merchandise is placed for sale.

BENEFIT: (WOW) What a feature of your product or service actually does for the buyer.

BOOK: Official company policy, often in written form, as in the book says no vacation time during July.

BIG PICTURE: The view of the entire organization or plan of action.

BOTTOM TO TOP SELLING: Selling technique that takes the customer to the bottom of the line or least expensive product first, then moves him up to a more expensive model. As example: "For only a few dollar more per month, you get all of theses extras, not offered on the base model." See also: Top to bottom selling.

BREAKEVEN POINT: When income and costs of doing business are equal. When a business breaks even.

BUDGET: A plan to allocate money, specifically where money comes from and how it will be spent.

CASE CUTTER: A metal sleeve that holds a single edge razor blade. A safety device used to cut open sealed cases of merchandise.

CO-OPERATIVE: (Co-op) An organization of small businesses, usually of the same type as in independent drug stores, with the intent to improve their purchasing power.

CO-OPERATIVE ADVERTISING: (Co-op Ads) When two or more retail stores, owned by different people, create joint advertising. Usually a circular to reduce costs.

COUPON: An advertising medium that offers consumers cash off when they buy a specific product within a specific market. This is done in place of a general price reduction.

COUPON DROP: The act of distributing a large number of cents off coupons to consumers. Usually in the form of direct mail.

CASH WITH ORDER: (CWO) Cash or a check is collected at the

time the order is written either because the account has bad credit or to take advantage of a cash discount.

CASH ON DELIVERY: (COD) Cash or check on delivery of goods. Common practice with rack jobbers or with those accounts with poor credit ratings.

CASH AND CARRY: A wholesale operation that doesn't provide delivery. The retailers go to the warehouse, pick out the goods they want and pay cash before leaving.

CASH COW: A business or product that has no outstanding debt and regularly delivers profit.

CERTIFIED CHECK WITH ORDER: With bad credit customers or with a new customer, a bank certified check is collected at the time the order is written. The customer can still stop a certified check. Always ask for cash from a poor payer.

CHAIN: A group of three stores or more that have one common owner or owners. (Two stores owned by one person don't constitute a chain in most industries.) A chain may be entitled to certain discounts from manufacturers that an independent isn't.

CIRCULAR: A printed advertising medium any where from 1 to

sixteen pages, that's mailed out to residences or handed out in the store.

CUT CASE: A method of displaying consumer goods, such as bottles of soda, by cutting the cases to expose the front of the product and stacking the cases on top of each other.

CHAIN OF COMMAND: The communication link from the lowest level of and organization to the highest level. As in the expression, "Never break the chain of command." Meaning never by-pass your immediate supervisor to register a complaint or offer a suggestion to his supervisor.

CHAIN STORE: Three or more stores owned by one person or group or corporation.

CLOSED ENDED QUESTION: A question that extracts a yes or no answer. As in: "Do you own a car?"

COMMUNICATION: The act of transmitting information orally, visually or in written form from one person to another.

COMMUNICATION BARRIER: Anything that prevents the transmission of information.

DEAD SPACE: Unused floor space in a retail store.

DISCONTINUED ITEM: When a retailer or manufacturer no longer carries an item. The retailer may discontinue it, but not the manufacturer.

DOLLAR COST AVERAGING: The consistent purchase of a product over time despite fluctuation in cost. The average cost is determined by the total amount spent divided by the total number of units purchased. As in, "I bought $100 worth of company stock every month for ten years. The price fluctuated from $6 a share to $15. I own 1,000 shares. The dollar cost average is $9.50 per share. Today's market value is $12.75 per share.

DOWN TIME: Time in which a machine isn't in operation producing. Sometimes used to refer to people who aren't productive as in, "He has too much down time."

ECONOMY OF SCALE: The greater the volume, the lower the per unit cost.

END USER: The person at the end of the pipeline who consumes or uses the product. A can of coffee may go through six hands to reach the marketplace. The person who drinks the coffee is the end user.

FACING: The number of positions an item has on the shelf. One size of peppermint mouthwash, three across, has three facings.

FEATURE: (SO WHAT!) An aspect of your product or service. "This car has fuel injection."

FILL IN ORDER: A small order to tie a retailer over until a regular shipment comes in.

FRANCHISE: A business licensed from a manufacturer or corporation by an individual with permission to use the manufacturer's name and logo. A contractual agreement.

FULL LINE FORCED: When a manufacturer forces a retailer to carry his full line of merchandise.

GATEKEEPER: Anyone assigned to screen visitors or advertising materials before other office personnel see them. Usually the receptionist is the first level gatekeeper and the office manager is the second level. If, in your private life you bring the mail in each day, discarding the junk mail and advertising circulars so no one else sees them, then you're the family gatekeeper.

GIVE-AWAYS: Advertising items with the company name, logo or product embossed on them. The purpose is to keep the brand in front of the decision-maker's eye. A type of subliminal advertising. Items include, pads, pens, coffee mugs and tee shirts. Items are given away at no charge by reps to secretaries, office staff and to buyers.

GOOD GUY / BAD GUY ROUTINE: Management strategy in which one day a manager acts as your best friend and the next day, act as though he's ready to fire you. This is intended to keep the sales force off balance and insecure. A variation is a consistently friendly 1st level manager and a consistently unfriendly second level manager. This is to keep the sales force in debt to the good manager for keeping the bad manager off their backs.

GUARANTEED SALES: A contract in which a supplier promises a refund for any merchandise he sold to a retailer that doesn't sell in a given amount of time.

HIGH PERCEIVER OF RISK: One who is very cautious and sees danger around every bend. One who afraid to try new ideas or products. One who is overly concerned with safety.

HOUSE ORGAN: An employer sponsored newsletter specifically for the benefit of the employees.

IMPULSE SALES: An unplanned purchase.

INITIAL ORDER: The first order a customer ever gives you.

INDEPENDENT: A small business that isn't owned by any other organization or chain store.

LINE EXTENSION: Increasing the number of selections of a product by adding new sizes, flavors or styles.

LOGO: A company's registered trademark.

LOSS LEADER: An item promoted below cost to attract customers.

LOW PERCEIVER OF RISK: One who sees little danger in any venture. One who thinks nothing bad can happen to them. One who is willing to take chances without fear of retribution. A skydiver is an example.

MANAGEMENT BY FEAR: (MBF) Intentional management style of motivating employees by threatening them with their jobs or merit raises. The most destructive style of management for a company and practiced by those least capable of effective management.

MANAGEMENT BY OBJECTIVE: (MBO) Setting specific objectives for a subordinate to follow.

MANAGEMENT BY EXAMPLE: (MBE) Demonstrating sales techniques to a subordinate in the field. As in a manger having a new rep watch him cover his territory and sell.

MANAGEMENT HYPE: When presenting a new program to the sales force, management tends to disregard negatives, stress only the positives and exaggerate claims.

ME TOO PRODUCT: A copycat product. When a company copies another successful product to cash in on its popularity.

MICROMANAGEMENT: When a manager closely supervises the day-to-day activities of his subordinates. Used by companies who hire inexperienced employees or recent graduates. Destructive when used on highly motivated employees. A weak management style.

OPEN-ENDED QUESTION: A question that extracts more than a yes or no answer. e.g.: What is the nature of your business?

OPEN TO BUY: A time frame in which a buyer places orders. He buys until his given budget runs out. First come, first served.

OUT OF STOCK: When a retailer or manufacturer no longer has an item available for sale and is awaiting a reorder.

PIPELINE: Means the pathway in which product flows from the manufacturer to the retailer to the consumer. As in we resolved the problem and got the retailer back in the pipeline.

OVERSTOCK: When a retailer or manufacturer has more inventory than they can sell in a reasonable amount of time.

PRIVATE LABEL: A store's own brand of a product.

PRODUCT OF CHOICE: The preferred brand of a consumer.

PROMOTIONAL MONEY: Money given or rebated to a retailer for advertising and displaying their product.

RAPPORT SELLING: Technique of befriending the buyer so you can trade on that friendship to get orders.

RETURN ON INVESTMENT: (ROI) The amount of profit returned in exchange for investment dollars. The strategy defined as, "It's not how much money you make, but how fast you make it."

REORDER POINT: A minimal level of inventory at which new product must be ordered to avoid an out of stock situation.

SLOT FEE: A fee large retailers charge to vendors to place merchandise on the shelf.

STRATEGY OF CHOICE: The process by which you offer a buyer the choice between two or more options, other than "yes" or "no." As an example: Rather than, "Do you want to buy this?" Ask, "I could have delivered Tuesday, or would Wednesday be better?"

STOCK KEEPING UNIT (SKU): One unit of merchandise. If a manufacturer makes five sizes of shampoo, each size counts as one SKU. If each makes five sizes in three different types he has fifteen SKUs. A retailer may elect to carry the seven most popular SKUs in his store.

STOCK ROTATION: The practice of placing newer inventory behind older inventory. This prevents merchandise from sitting in the back room and going out of style or out of date.

TERRITORY REALIGNMENT: Change in your present territory that shifts its boundaries to make it larger or smaller.

TERRITORY EXPANSION: When a company adds more reps to its sales force thereby reducing the size of everyone's territory or by expanding into new areas.

TOP TO BOTTOM SELLING: When the most expensive model is offered to a customer first in hopes that they may buy it. When the seller moves down the line to less expensive models in hopes the buyer would take a more expensive model than he otherwise would have if they started from the bottom and worked up.

UNIVERSAL PRODUCT CODE: The ten-digit code and bar graph used to identify the manufacturer, product size and flavor of a product. Used in scanners for checkout and ordering.

UNIT PRICING: State law requiring retailers to post unit pricing for each item to aid consumers in price comparison.

WANT LIST: A list a retailer keeps of items requested by customers.

ABOUT THE AUTHOR

I am a native of Greenville, South Carolina. I attended The School of Visual Arts in New York where I studied Advertising Copywriting, Art and Design. I graduated from Adelphi University with a degree in business and management. My career path includes experience as both field trainer and a sales representative. I live on Long Island; have a beautiful wife and three beautiful daughters and three grandchildren. I teach classes at Nassau Community College on publishing, Advertising Copywriting and Sales. In addition, I do volunteer work at the Cradle of Aviation Museum on Long Island.

Other books include
Study Guide for the US Immigration Test in 8 languages
The Sales Rep Survival Guide
Advertising Copywriting and the Unique Selling Proposition
The Bully Boss, a novel
A New York Wedding, a novel